How

ONE CUP

OF

COFFEE

Can Change Your
World

ROBERT THIBODEAU

Robert Thibodeau

ISBN:1724543644
ISBN-13:978-1724543646

DEDICATION

This book is dedicated to all of the men and women who put their life on the line, each and every day, so we can live in freedom. My military brothers and sisters will always hold a special place in my heart. To this day, every time I hear the National Anthem played, I still get a tear in my eye (and sometimes I even cry as I contemplate what this country means to me and to those I served with and to those who defend Her today). My many years of service in the military has shaped my life like no other thing. It is because of my military time, which gave birth to this book.

I also want to dedicate this book to my brothers and sisters in blue, not just police officers I have had the privilege to work with, but ALL first responders - I dedicate this book to you as well. Even though I have retired from Law Enforcement, I still keep on eye on an officers' "six" as I pass by on the highway (just making sure they are not in a fight or appear in distress). I consider it my duty to do so.

So, having said all of that, I want to dedicate this book **to YOU!** I want you to take this story and make it your own, just as I did when Major General Taylor first told this story in my presence back in 1988.

Take it – run with it – and go get that

"ONE CUP OF COFFEE!"

ACKNOWLEDGMENTS

Although he has long ago retired, then Major General James Taylor, Commander, 5th Infantry Division, Fort Polk, LA (1988-89) is the one that inspired me to take "One Cup of Coffee" and I have used it my entire life (and for this book).

I also want to acknowledge LTC J.P. Hogan, who was the Squadron Commander of the 3rd Squadron, 1st Cavalry Division, whom I served under during the time where this little piece of wisdom was imparted. I was LTC Hogan's S-3 (Air) during this time. He also helped to calm the waters as I was making a transition from military to civilian life. I have always thought of myself as a life-long CAV Trooper, even after ending my military career and transitioning into my civilian life.

And of course, my good friend Sean Douglas, author, speaker and podcaster (www.TheSuccessCorps.com) who has kept me motivated to "tell my story." Sean and I have very similar backgrounds and I treasure his wisdom in helping me to get my story out to the world.

This book is just one part of that story. But it is one story worth sharing. This one thing has inspired me and helped me for the last 30 years. I hope it does the same for you.

Robert Thibodeau

Robert Thibodeau

CONTENTS

Robert Thibodeau

Chapter One
Background of "Making Coffee"

On a training mission in the mid-1980's, while part of the 3rd Squadron of the 1st US Cavalry Division, part of the US Army's 5th Infantry Division...we had just finished a Brigade v. Brigade simulated combat mission.

Our Squadron had performed excellently. We had found, located and fixed the position of the enemy so well, that when the "battle" started (the Division Commander observing), the Artillery units effectively neutralized the enemy forces within minutes. About two hours after the "battle" started, the Division Commander stopped the action. This "battle" was supposed to take between two and three days to complete!

As part of our Squadron's S-3 (Planning and Operations) office, I was part of our Squadron Commander's team to attend the after-action review. Although I was not a presenter at this review, I was privileged to be in the Division TOC (Tactical Operations Command). I was the Squadron S-3 Air (responsible for Air to Ground Coordination). I was also the designated liaison officer and familiar with the Division TOC location. Therefore, our commander requested I attend also.

The briefing started with the Cavalry Commander (my commander) giving his briefing. On the large map of the area, he pinpointed almost every tank location on the map. All along the "front lines," he described the tank, the type of fighting position and, in some cases, locations of support units as well.

We had accomplished our mission, of what I called "sneak and peak" well. We had not been discovered and our scout units had accurately relayed the locations to our Squadron TOC.

The Brigade commander than gave his assessment, using the information the CAV had provided to his TOC. He went over how he had maneuvered his tank battalions and had used the artillery to support an attack that had totally wiped out the enemy units.

The "losing" Brigade commander then gave his briefing. He told about his locations and what his battle plan had been. In the end, he was taking some "ribbing" from the General and the other Brigade commander for the quick losses he had suffered. Everyone acknowledged it was because of the excellent work the Cavalry had accomplished.

Then, Major General James Taylor, the Division Commander, rose to speak. The words he stated, at first, bewildered me. But as he explained what he said, it resonated within me. They made so much sense. His short speech was so profound, that I vowed to use his example in everything I did. I have used it every training event while in service and I also used this concept successfully in business after I left the military. I have used this technique to also assist in the training of my police officers under my command when I was a police supervisor.

The General said, "Well, gentlemen, I can say one thing. *We made some coffee today. On both sides. Let me explain..."*

And what he shared, I now share with you...just modified from the military point of view so you can use it in your business.

Let's get started...

Chapter Two

MAKING COFFEE FOR YOUR BUSINESS

(No Matter What Your Business Is)

No matter what your business is. No matter where you are located. No matter if you are brick and mortar store or an online e-business. You can do better. You know you can.

You try hard. You do all of the right things (at least what you think are the right things to do). But it never works the way you expected it to work.

Sometimes, the smallest detail can make the difference between a huge success and a mediocre failure. Why is that?

No matter the business you are in, you MUST first analyze the CRITICAL steps that are necessary for you to win. What are the key components that MUST be present for you to win? These are the keys which you must make sure are in place - in every circumstance and at all times.

It could range from product development to product

launch. From an advertising campaign to receiving orders. From generating leads to closing sales. From product payment to product delivery. From answering customer questions to customer service after the sale. The key components are endless and depend entirely on the business you are building.

But, you must actually sit down and discover (or decide upon) only the key elements that MUST be present for you to win. Once you have accomplished that one step (and ONLY when that one step is accomplished), will you be able to proceed to make your cup of coffee!

Chapter Three

Making COFFEE for Your Organization

The commanding general, in the illustration I laid out in the beginning, spoke about "making coffee." The way he explained it was a technique to identify the great results that were obtained by one side in the mock battle and also, at the same time, to give the "losing Brigade Commander some complements as well. He was able to help the other brigade commander to leave the after action briefing feeling as if he had truly accomplished something in the battle as well. The general made a training session out of what happened. We can do the same for you.

Once you have the KEY ELEMENTS of your situation, business or even your department (if within a larger organization) – it is just a matter of "mixture" that will produce the desired results.

In making coffee, you have just a couple of key elements.

1. **COFFEE**
2. **WATER**
3. **A CONTAINER**
4. **HEAT**

Those are the key elements needed to make any cup of coffee.

If you have too much coffee and not enough water – it is bitter coffee. But you still have coffee.

If you have too much water and not enough coffee – it is weak coffee.

If you have enough coffee and enough water but no pot to heat the water in – you do not have coffee.

If you have enough coffee and enough water and the pot to heat the water in – but NO HEAT source – you do not have coffee.

BUT – when you have the right amount of coffee and the correct amount of water and the pot to heat the water in AND the heat source...you can enjoy a GREAT CUP OF COFFEE!

So, the question is: How can you figure out how to make coffee for your team?

Great Question! (I should have thought of that one myself)!

Let's look at how you can make:

Your Perfect Cup of Coffee!

Chapter Four

Finding Out How To Make

YOUR Perfect Cup of Coffee

First, identify the key components that would make you successful. Don't focus on other companies or other departments that you have no control over. Focus ONLY on what you are responsible for.

If you are the business owner, identify the different departments within your organization. Identify what the DESIRED END RESULT is for your business. Don't be shy. Write down specifics! If you cheat and fudge here, you will only be cheating yourself (and you may NEVER make a "good cup of coffee")!

For example: Let's make you a fictional company. For purposes of this example, you are now the owner of a janitorial service. You need the following **specific** jobs in order to operate your company.

1. Sales – obtain clients.
2. Customer Service – set the most convenient time for the janitorial services to be completed. (Some businesses want this service in the overnight hours, some first thing in the morning, etc.).

3. Supply Department – make sure there are adequate janitorial supplies for the work force to accomplish their tasks on a daily basis.
4. Cleaning Staff – depending on the size of this department, you may need to appoint a Cleaning Staff Manager to hold the rest of the staff accountable.
5. Billing Department – ensures clients are billed accurately and that clients are paying their invoices promptly.
6. Payroll Department – not involved in customer service or in Billing / Collections. ONLY involved in generating an accurate payroll, with all appropriate taxes collected from paychecks and paid, as required, to the government. Also, ensure all staff are paid accurately and on time.
7. Management – holds each department accountable for their required duties.

Now, I just made that up. I have never been involved in janitorial service (except when I was a private in the Army. I became an expert at cleaning EVERYTHING – often with a toothbrush)!

But, I believe it represents an accurate picture of what a successful janitorial services company would look like. You probably have a different company – but you can identify with what I just laid out in the example.

Now, your job is to sit down and give the

BIG, OVERVIEW PICTURE of your company!

Do not get into specifics about each area that needs to be accomplished (for example: I could go into the SALES item and list – 6 outside sales staff paid hourly base rate plus commission. They are required to call on 12 business every day and turn in documentation of these sales calls. These sales people must follow up every two weeks with new contacts, etc. etc. etc.). Do you see how I could get bogged down doing that?

So DON'T DO THAT!

Leave that to your department head as he/she makes "their" cup of coffee for their department's area of responsibility!

Get the 10,000-foot overview of your organization! That is what you are looking at as we proceed to the next chapter.

Robert Thibodeau

Chapter Five

WORKSHEET: What Is Your

10,000 Foot Overview?

1. Type of Business You Are Operating (or Planning to Operate):

2. What is the END RESULT for the consumer?

3. How can YOU provide the END RESULT for the Consumer?

4. Why Should the Consumer Hire YOU? (HINT: What do you do better than anyone else?):

5. Taking your answer to #4, Explain how that is part of your answer to #3:

6. Taking your answer in #5, combine your answer with #1 and #2 and write a paragraph that would explain it to a client or potential client:

Chapter Six

MY EXAMPLE FOR THE

JANITORIAL SERVICE COMPANY

The numbers below correspond to the questions in the Worksheet for my fictional Janitorial Company:

#1: Provide Janitorial Services to businesses and office complexes in the "XYZ City area".

#2: To operate a clean work environment for their employees and customers.

#3: We can operate on a 24-hour basis servicing our clients at their preferred time of day, 7 days per week. We have teams of 3 people and one supervisor to quickly and efficiently clean the office areas. The supervisor is there to work with the client for special areas of interest or areas that need to be attended to immediately.

#4: We use state of the art vacuuming and floor scrubbing equipment. This equipment uses biodegradable cleaning agents that are safe to the environment but also are super effective at cleaning surfaces. All of our cleaning products reduce office allergies and make surfaces sparkle again. Our floor cleaning products will bring the shine back to heavily worn traffic areas in tile and will lift even the toughest stains from carpets.

#5: We can provide a quick cleanup during the daytime when office personnel are present. This service will clean all counters, rest rooms, lunch areas and hallways. Individual offices will be cleaned during the overnight hours (preferred). The heavy duty cleaning team can have your entire office cleaned from "top to bottom and all the way around" during the overnight hours.

Our team of 4 people (one is an onsite supervisor) will sanitize the common areas where germs love to hide out! We can have the counters, desktops, hallways and rest rooms sparkling clean. The carpeted areas will be treated and given a deep down cleaning with our new, state of the art vacuuming and cleaning equipment. All of our cleaning materials are biodegradable and help to reduce allergens that live in office complexes. We can even clean the ventilation vents and windows.

#6: We are a state of the art janitorial service specializing in servicing the cleaning needs of "XYZ City's" best businesses and office complex workspaces. Our only purpose is to provide a clean, allergy and germ free working environment for your employees and clients. We can provide a quick cleanup during the daytime when office personnel are present. This service will clean all counters, rest rooms, lunch areas and hallways. Individual offices will be cleaned during the overnight hours (preferred). The heavy duty cleaning team can have your entire office cleaned from top to bottom and all the way around during the overnight hours. Our team of 4 people (one is an onsite supervisor) will sanitize the common areas where germs love to hide out! We can have the counters, desktops, hallways and rest rooms sparkling clean. The carpeted areas will be treated and given a deep down cleaning with our new, state of the art vacuuming and cleaning equipment. All of our cleaning materials are biodegradable and help to reduce allergens that live in office complexes. We can even clean the ventilation vents and windows!

Congratulations! ***You have now completed the hardest part of this course!*** The rest of what we will talk about will allow you to fine tune the end result of the work you did above!

Robert Thibodeau

Chapter Seven

Identify Your Key Players In

Each of Your Critical Areas

You now must decide what are the critical components of your business. Generalities will not do here. The lower you can go, "niching down" in every area, will work wonders in how quickly your business will grow.

Do not try to be easy on yourself in this section. Be honest and admit that you do not know everything there is to know about your business. **Come on! Admit it!** Write in the space below these exact words: "I (write your name), admit to myself, I do not know everything there is to know about my business!"

Write it here:

Now, sign your name here:

_____

Enter today's date here:

_____

Now, in your own words, "Why did you have to write those exact words?" Enter your response here:

_____

_____

You should have entered something to the effect of:

"I wrote the above statement to remind me that I do not have all of the answers to all of the problems that I face in my business."

Very good - Let's proceed...

Write your type of business (in our example: Janitorial Services):

Now, what will it take for you to find and service ONE CLIENT?

(Do not go listing out individual job duties or supply items. Just enter what it will take, as far as human resources, equipment and TIME to service one client):

Next, take your list and combine items and areas until you have, at a minimum three and at a maximum FOUR items:

Item or area #1:

Item or area #2:

Item or area #3:

Item or area #4:

These are the areas where you SHOULD BE focusing your attention in order to be successful in your business. YOU only need to focus on these areas! That's it!

I can hear the question already... *"But I have sub-areas within each of those major areas!"*

YES! That's the answer! Don't you see?

As the business owner, your focus is to only be on the major areas. *You need to hire people to help you with* *the sub-areas!*

If you place a responsible person in charge of ONE major area, you will end up with FOUR EMPLOYEES (or volunteers – especially in non-profits). These will be your office managers for those respective areas!

Let's go back to our example of the janitorial service company.

I had six major areas plus a seventh called "Management." Since the most I can have is four areas...and one of them MUST BE "Management," I need to combine the other six into three areas. How can I accomplish this? Let's look at the six:

Sales   **Customer Service**   **Supplies**

Cleaning Staff   **Billing**   **Payroll**

What three areas could I combine these departments into?

Well, Sales and Customer Service should be working together.

The cleaning staff and supply department rely on each other.

Billing and payroll could also be combined.

So now, my Major Departments are:

Sales/Customer Service

Cleaning Staff and Supplies

Billing and Payroll

Then, when I add in the 7th area – **MANAGEMENT**, I find that I really do not need a "management staff." I can appoint a responsible person in each of those departments to be the department supervisor.

This, in effect, gives someone a promotion and a pay raise to go with the extra duties. I now have a MANAGEMENT STAFF that I can hold accountable!

We have just identified the four components we need to MAKE COFFEE for our organization!

Look at it like this:

Without "Sales and Customer Service" – *we have no new clients or returning clients.* We are not going to be in business long.

Without Cleaning Staff or Supplies for them to use – *we will not be in business long.*

Without Billing and Payroll, we will not know who owes us what amount of money and we will not know which sales personnel to pay. *We will not be able to pay ANY of* *workforce* – which means, we will not be in business long.

And without somebody in each department that we can hold accountable for the performance of their department – *we will not be in business long!*

We have correctly identified the Key Components to make coffee for our organization.

Next up – let's look at the different "mixtures" that are necessary for us to make GOOD COFFEE!

Chapter Eight

The First Thing You Need is –

COFFEE!

You must have some COFFEE grounds before you can make COFFEE. That makes sense, right?

If you have a pot, but no water or heat, you just have a pot...

If you have water, but nothing to put the water in and no heat source, you just have "wet coffee..."

If you have heat, but no pot or water, you just have burned coffee...

Each of these are interdependent on the others...

The only common element that must be present in each of these scenarios - **is COFFEE!**

So, the very first thing we need is the COFFEE.

Depending on taste, some people like dark roast and some medium or even light roast. Some like COFFEE from different parts of the world and some like their COFFEE from only one area of the world.

In your business, the first thing you need to decide upon

is what can be termed as **"THE MOST IMPORTANT THING."** This is what you must give most of your focus and attention to.

This should also be part of the **"Mission Statement"** for your organization.

This way, you make sure every person in your organization is aware of **"What the Most Important Thing"** is to you! This part MUST be in your COFFEE mixture or you will just be "boiling water" at best (and if you just boil water without adding the coffee – eventually, the pot runs dry! And that is what will happen to your business without the primary ingredient: **COFFEE).**

In our example company, the primary ingredient would be the Mission Statement. For example:

"We provide a clean, allergy and germ free working environment for your employees and clients by providing janitorial services at a time that is convenient for you."

You need to make banners with this mission statement (yes, more than one). You should make this the default screen saver on all computers. You should have this on your company letterhead. You should have it on all business cards and stationary. You should have it on...*(you pick)!*

This keeps it in front of your employees AND your clients!

Everyone will know what it is you do and what he or she can expect if they choose you to be their janitorial service provider.

In your business, what is the ONE THING that defines you as a company? What is the ONE THING – the MOST IMPORTANT THING – **that you want people to know about your company?**

Many business owners want to be known for all of the different types of services they have and how they can cater to every company on an individual basis. They want to be the *"al a carte"* of their industry.

The problem with this type of thinking is that, in most cases, they are still only known for "one service." If one of your clients is speaking to a business associate and the conversation turns towards the cleanliness of the facility (in our example company), do you think your client will give a laundry list of things you do? **No.**

In fact, if the question were posed as, "Your business seems so clean! I mean, this place smells great too! How are you able to do that?"

The response is, "We have "XYZ Janitorial come in three times per week in the evenings. They handle all of that. We love 'em! Do you want their business card? I can hook you up."

The response is not, *"XYZ Janitorial is a janitorial service company that uses only allergen free cleaning supplies. Their services range from **(blah, blah, blah, blah, blah)."***

SO – only focus on THE MAJOR THING that you want your clients to remember about you. Especially when they are talking to others about your company!

Here are some examples...give me your responses to the right of these branding slogans:

"Good to the last drop..." _____

"Finger lickin' good..."   _____

"Taste the rainbow..."   _____

"Snap, Crackle, Pop..."   _____

"Just Do It..."   _____

I know those are advertising slogans and not mission statements. But using this analogy, you can see what I mean. Those slogans serve to bring the company's name to the memory of the person who hears it.

Your **"Most Important Thing"** should do the same thing for your clients. They NEED to know this! Your employees NEED TO KNOW THIS.

YOU NEED TO KNOW THIS!

Everything else must revolve around

"YOUR MOST IMPORTANT THING!"

Agreed?

Ok, let's move on!

Robert Thibodeau

Chapter Nine

Next Important Thing:

Is it the Pot, The Water or The Heat?

So we have established the other three major elements as a container – the Pot; the water and the heat. They are all interdependent, although separate items.

In our janitorial services company, we have three major categories plus Management. Let's look at the three areas again:

Sales/Customer Service

Cleaning Staff and Supplies

Billing and Payroll

If you try to make a janitorial services company and ONLY build a Sales team without Customer Support...or you combine these into a single department, but you do not have a cleaning staff or supplies – you will not have a successful company.

Or if you just have a cleaning staff and supplies, but no sales or support staff – you will spend all day trying to knock on doors and clean offices in the day time (and probably 2/3 or more of your customers will want cleaning after hours. So you lose out on this huge block of business).

Or if you only have a billing department but no sales staff and no cleaning teams out there doing business...your plans are failing from the start!

So we see all three of these areas are totally interdependent on the success of the other groups!

But, we also need a Management team to keep all of the other areas working in coordination together. If the other three departments just go out running on their own – they have no idea if the other departments are going on vacation or going to work!

So the Management team must be the coordinator that keeps all of the other three departments working together. The amount of input the Management team gives the other departments will affect how well they are going to perform. And their performance is totally relying on the success of the departments other than their own.

With our COFFEE analogy, we know we have to have COFFEE in order to "make coffee," correct? Without coffee, the best you can have is hot water.

Definitely NOT COFFEE!

The amount of input the management team provides determines how well the other departments work together.

Just the right amount of COFFEE will make a perfect product. If you add too much coffee because you want "more caffeine" in the morning – you may get the extra caffeine, but the coffee will be bitter and just plain "nasty!"

Too much input by management will have the same effect – it makes things NASTY! It may be well intentioned by the management team. It may be in an effort to increase the "stats" in a certain area. And it will work, in that area. But everything else is going to suffer.

Why is this the case?

When you focus too much attention on one area at the exclusion of the other areas, those other areas will suffer. They will not continue to increase; they will not continue to produce for you. It may not happen immediately, but it will happen. ***"Decrease cometh!"***

What if you have a limited amount of coffee, but you want extra cups of coffee (extra products; extra production in your company)?

Well, you will have the extra cups of coffee to distribute – but every single cup you pass out will be WEAK COFFEE. Little more than hot, flavored water…

You will probably not have people knocking on your door for refills. You may even see people pouring it out on the ground!

Your good intentions ended up turning people off!

So you cannot keep your resources the same and expect more production. *(Boy, could some of the places I worked at learn a lot from that one statement)!* Your clients will not accept the end product.

In our Janitorial Services Company, if we want "more clients" – but we do not add more cleaning staff or buy more supplies, what will happen?

Let's look at that situation…

So, in our example, you have three teams.

First, your cleaning teams will begin to be overwhelmed. Instead of each team cleaning three businesses each evening, they need to clean five. This sounds good for your business, right?

Let's say you charge $200 for an office cleaning and you pay the teams $100. You spend $10 on cleaning supplies. You spend $40 on office staff and support.

Leaving $50 in profit.

So, if one team cleans three offices each night, you receive $150 in profit. Since you have three teams, this becomes $450 in profit each night. Five nights per week, $2250 per week profit!

Now, management makes the decision to increase from three to five business to clean each night, per team. ON PAPER, this will result in $250 profit per team per night. For three teams, this equates to $750 profit per night, $3750 profit per week for your business (this is after ALL the payroll is paid, including your salary).

This sounds like a great plan!

But soon, you find team members calling out sick more often. You see a higher turnover of employees. You start to receive more complaints in your customer service department. It seems some things are being missed during the cleanings. You find out the teams, instead of spending two hours per office cleaning, they are now spending 90 minutes. They need to hurry so they can get to the next building...and the next...and the next.

So, you start to lose clients...

You start to lose employees on the cleaning teams...

Moral is going down...

Sick leave time is going up...

Expenses are going up...

And the income revenue is not coming in as projected...

WHY?

Because management decided to "add too much coffee" to the mix!

And this made the coffee unbearable, NASTY!

Too much coffee sounds like it will work...but it doesn't. You still made coffee – it was just too strong!

Chapter Ten

Too Much Water

(not enough coffee)

If you add too much water when trying to make coffee, your end result is little more than flavored water. Not very appealing to look at. Even worse to taste.

In our example above, it was stated that some would be poured out on the ground. Your efforts to appease the masses has not worked.

How does this relate to our business? How does this relate to "making coffee?"

Well, you must decide "who your ideal client" is going to be. This is the person that you must center your entire business around. This is what is commonly called your "avatar."

For example: If you are making shoes. Are you going to make ladies shoes or men's shoes? Are you going to make athletic shoes or dress shoes? Are you going to make casual shoes or formal shoes? If you answered "All the above" – you are on your way to making *"weak" coffee.*

It looks good on paper to list all of the different categories you can provide to the public. But most of the public is not going to purchase shoes from you! You need to narrow your niche down to one or two products *(at least in the beginning)*.

If you want to focus only on producing athletic shoes for women, your avatar is not going to be a 65-year-old lady who is attending a formal ball event. Your avatar is not going to be a 45-year old house wife who needs a pair of shoes for a wedding.

Your avatar is not going to be 35-year old executive who needs a pair of dress shoes for work.

Do you see how you need to focus on one or two different ideas - but only ONE avatar?

You may decide on producing athletic shoes for women. You may have one product line for women doing aerobic workouts and one product line for runners. You need to focus all of your attention and marketing of your products to one specific avatar.

Your avatar might be a marathon runner, 28 years old, married, a mother and employed. She has to manage her training runs into her already packed schedule. She needs a pair of shoes that will last the entire running season. She needs a pair of shoes that will absorb much of the shock, which the feet, shins and knees take during running. She needs a pair of breathable shoes that will allow the sweat to evaporate through the shoes (and air our quickly after a run). She also needs a pair of shoes that do not look like a 1950's throw back to "tennis shoes." She wants something stylish but functional at the same time.

WOW!

You now have an actionable plan on designing your first product line! It may take you a while to get this product up and running *(excuse the pun).* But while you are going through this process – start your marketing campaign.

Take advantage of every opportunity to "get your name out there." Develop a marketing strategy around your avatar. Where would *she* "hang out?" Where would *she* shop? What events would *she* participate in? Where would *she* train?

What events would *she* sign up for as practice runs?

Once you identify those things, you should develop a marketing plan to put your name into those locations!

You might have a tent at running events and give away little gadgets, etc. with your name and logo on them. You might have towels made and put into the "goodie bags" given to runners.

Once you have some initial products produced, advertise at these events and ask for "beta testers" to run with your shoes and to give you feedback. "GIVE AWAY" those shoes to those who agree to participate. Plus give away a credit voucher for a future pair of shoes when the final version comes to market.

Get them to give you testimonials after they finish their race. Video tape them (if possible). Good or bad – keep them and thank them for their input.

If someone did not like your shoes, take that back to the marketing and development team and determine "why." Maybe the person was too heavy for your shoes. Maybe they needed an extra wide version. Or a narrower version.

The point being, <u>do not just dismiss a negative review!</u> Just like you share the positive reviews – share the negative reviews *(with your team)* and analyze why the person did not like them. If you can adapt your product line to fix that problem – great! If it is something that was a "one time occurrence," then dismiss it.

The point I am trying to make in this example is very simple. Identify WHO your ideal client is. Then center everything you do on catering to that one person. You will have some people that drift into your market from other directions. Those are great! But DO NOT try to expand your market to those other avatar's until you are truly satisfied that your primary client avatar is being 100% served by your company!

Only then should you begin to expand your product line. But you need to go through the same steps with each category of client you are trying to capture.

Remember – **"Too much water and not enough coffee"** just results in **bad tasting flavored water!** Make sure you have enough coffee for the amount of water you are going to use. Know your client. **Serve your client – one cup of coffee at a time, if necessary.** At least you will have a loyal following!

And that is what will expand your business.

Robert Thibodeau

Chapter Eleven

Too Much Heat

"Will Burn the Coffee"

Heat here can be compared to the amount of oversight the management staff provides to the sales force. Too much is not good. Too little is even worse. You must get it "just right!" Just like a good cup of coffee will not be too hot nor will it be lukewarm. It will be "just right."

When management (meaning you and your direct supervisors) interacts with the workers, there is a tendency on the part of the workers to think you are spying on them! You cannot help that your presence may make them feel uncomfortable. Especially if you are "providing verbal guidance" on how they should perform their jobs.

If you are putting pressure on your supervisors (your management staff), the lower ranking employees will also sense that pressure. At first, your orders will be complied with. **But rebellion will soon come.** If not through the workers, it will come through your management staff as they begin to disregard your instructions. The reason: **_They are "protecting" their subordinates._** And do you want to know the worst part?

They are protecting them

FROM YOU!

Now, knowing this, how are you going to make sure everything is being done the way you feel it should be accomplished? Easy...you meet with the supervisors at your office location (not on site where the workers are). In these meetings, you should discuss any problems or situations the management team is facing. Any problem areas with the clients? Any problem areas with the workers?

You then address some joint solutions to any issues and problems. You do not "tell them" how to do their jobs! You ask for their input and then guide them, collectively, to the solution!

Ask how they believe the issue should be addressed and solved. Don't push your answer on them. Allow them to voice some ideas and, if different than yours, walk them through, step by step, to see if it really would work. **Sometimes, the "boots on the ground" know more than the "boss in the chair."**

The reason you have them as your management staff is for this very reason. So use them to discuss and work out any problems into a **win-win-win _for you, your client and your employees._**

Chapter Twelve

Too Much Coffee and

Not Enough Heat

Well, as you can imagine, all you managed to do is make some "mud." I suppose you could make the case for "ice coffee." But are you trying to "fire up" your services or put the flames out?

We are talking about making a great cup of coffee!

Get the mixture correct and you will have people lining up to get ahold of your coffee!

It does not matter what your niche is. If you are providing a great product or service; one that is in demand; one that is impactful; one that is needed – you will have people lining up to "purchase your coffee product."

But, if you slack off in any of your four fundamental areas, you will begin to lose your cliental. You will begin to lose money. You may even lose your business.

Stay focused on the four fundamental parts (which you discovered earlier) of your business. Make everything you do revolve around the accomplishment of these four areas. You could even make your management staff (on site supervisors in our example) coordinate together, develop and present to you their recommendations on how to handle any problem areas they identify.

Being in a position to do that will work wonders towards you achieving success in your chosen line of work! Use the management staff to handle on site emergencies, general oversight of the job and to bring to you – not just problems – but thoughtful, possible outcomes that will FIX the problems!

Now, let me address a very sensitive area.

Workers are always going to complain. It does not matter what the job is, they will complain. I've dealt with privates complaining about their sergeants; I've dealt with sergeants complaining about their officers; I've dealt with insurance agents complaining about office staff; I've dealt with police officers complaining about Headquarters staff and Headquarters staff complaining about Detachment staff and the patrol officers!

Here is a tip that I have used extensively in my long and varied career. It works no matter the job and no matter the skill level of the workers. If you enforce it every time a complaint is brought to your attention, **it WILL stop**

most of the frivolous complaints you have to listen to.

I simply tell the person who is doing the complaining, *"How do you recommend we fix this problem?"*

Almost immediately, you will see a look of confusion come upon their face! They were not expecting that response!

As they start to stammer, make and hold direct eye contact and simply say, *"I can tell you have thought long and hard about this area* (which they are complaining about), *so I am interested in hearing what your ideas are on how to improve? Tell me, how do you recommend we fix this situation?"*

As the person is now reeling a bit, stammering and trying to figure out something intelligent to say, reinforce your position by saying to them (and if they brought this up in a public setting, say this as well in the same public setting), *"If you want to bring me a problem, I expect you to also offer me two or maybe three well thought out solutions to the problem."*

Then turn and walk away...

It WORKS! I've used it on numerous occasions.

To give credit where credit is due, I learned this the "hard way" from LTC John Purvis IV when I was a young

2nd Lieutenant in the 4th Squadron 12th Cavalry.

LTC Purvis was tough as nails...and feared by officers and NCO's alike. He did not like to entertain "BS" – and he did not like to hear complaining. But, if you brought him a problem and offered a solution, he would jump into action to fix the problem. When he put you on the spot, you had better not try to "BS" him, because he was right more times than not!

My point being, **YOU are the boss.** YOU will make the decisions of how and what your employee's should do. YOU do not need to waste your valuable time to listen to frivolous complaining (needless to say your employee's valuable time when they could be doing actual work)!

When you finally get your staff operating like that – you have made a **WONDERFUL CUP OF COFFEE!**

Now, it's time to sit back and take a sip of some real coffee! You deserve it!

Chapter Thirteen

SUMMARY

You can apply the "One Cup of Coffee" analogy to just about any situation or any business model you can think of. You can use it in your personal relationships or in business; you can use it in your education or in purchasing stocks and bonds. This "One Cup of Coffee" analogy is applicable to just about any situation!

And that is what it should be – right? I mean, who can argue when you are only asking them to just sit down with you and talk - over

"One Cup of Coffee."

I think we have seen, *it really can change your world!*

Robert Thibodeau

Chapter Fourteen

About the Author

Robert Thibodeau

Robert Thibodeau, or Bob – as he likes to be called – is a retired police officer for a Maryland State Police Agency; he is a former US Army Cavalry Officer; a business entrepreneur and has been an Ordained Minister since 2001.

He currently heads the operation of an online Christian Radio Station, "Evangelism Radio," that has been rated by Shoutcast.com as #1 in the world in their genre on several occasions. The radio station has over 50 different ministries providing weekly content, with listeners in over 160 different nations.

He hosts the podcast "Kingdom Cross Roads Podcast," which is an interview based podcast with over 300 episodes in the last 18 months or so (at the time of this writing). On the podcast, Bob interviews pastors, ministers, Christian authors, musicians, business professionals and other Podcasters as well. He now has over 20K downloads during the first 18 months the podcast has been active (again, at the time of this writing).

Bob is also an Inspirational Speaker and a Leadership Coach. Contact him to schedule him to speak to your group or to assist you in Leadership Training or Team Building.

SOCIAL MEDIA HANDLES

If you have questions, comments or need help getting started in online radio broadcasting or in podcasting, please contact Robert Thibodeau at his email below. Be sure to put in the Subject Line: **"Question from your Book"** in order to capture his attention *(due to the number of emails he receives on a daily basis).*

Facebook: *https://www.facebook.com/ftfministries*

Twitter: *@bob_thibodeau*

LinkedIn: *www.linkedin.com/in/bob-thibodeau-speaks*

Email: *brotherbob@ftfm.org*

Websites

Personal: *www.bobthibodeau.com*

Ministry: *www.ftfm.org*

Radio Station: *www.evangelismradio.com*

   Evangelism Radio Twitter: *@evangelismradio*

Podcast: *www.kcrpodcast.com*

Other Books Written by Robert Thibodeau

All of these books are available on **Amazon.com** and can also be ordered through your favorite, local bookstore. You can also visit our websites to purchase through the website directly.

T.E.A.M. Training – How to Increase Your Profitability While Decreasing Stress and Employee Turnover

Blind Faith – How To Receive What You Cannot See

7 Keys to Answered Prayer

Six Trials of Jesus

www.ingramcontent.com/pod-product-compliance
Lightning Source LLC
Chambersburg PA
CBHW071237220526
45468CB00002B/889